FAIRIES

Written and Illustrated By Robert Newland

www.darkdorset.co.uk

First published in 2006 by S. B. Publications
Tel: 01323 893498
Email: sbpublications@tiscali.co.uk

ISBN 1-85770-315-4

Designed and Typeset by Robert Newland

Artwork by EH Graphics, East Sussex (01273) 515527

Contents

In the old days of King Arthur,
Of which Britons speak great honour,
All was this land filled with fairy,
The elf-queen with her jolly company.

Chaucer: *Canterbury Tales*

'As we faced each other on the path, I marvelled at the perfection of her tiny body. Like all the others, she was ten or so inches high, slender-hipped, bare-footed, and buck naked. Whether she was old or young I could not tell. There was no hair on her body, except for the head, where it was fair and very long. It floated down around her shoulders and her back obeying the very languid gravity in which she moved. Though neither brown nor white, her skin could not be described as a single colour at all. Like a beam of sunlight, she was all colours and no colour at all.

Observing this creature and her fellows gave me a visceral delight. She was so cunningly formed in every detail. So like a perfectly animated doll'.

Steve Szilagyi: *Photographing Fairies (1995)*

"I feel that the only true tales are fairy tales."

J. Foster Forbes: *The Unchronicled Past*

4

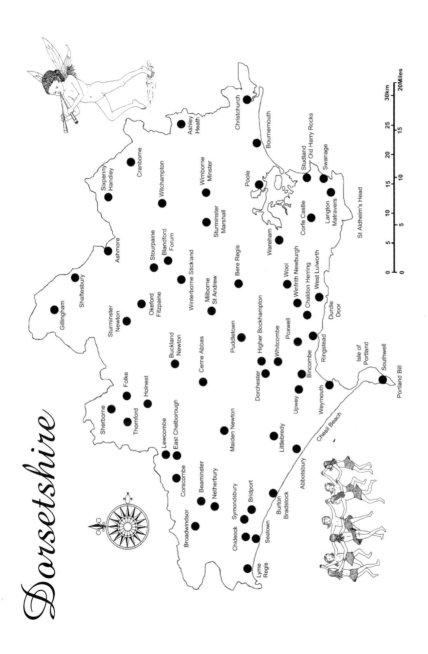

Dorsetshire

N

30km
20Miles

Gillingham
Shaftesbury
Sixpenny Handley
Cranborne
Ashley Heath
Christchurch
Bournemouth
Witchampton
Wimborne Minster
Sturminster Marshall
Poole
Studland
Old Harry Rocks
Swanage
Ashmore
Stourpaine
Blandford Forum
Bere Regis
Wareham
Corfe Castle
Langton Matravers
St Aldhelm's Head
Sturminster Newton
Okeford Fitzpaine
Winterborne Stickland
Milborne St Andrew
Wool
Winfrith Newburgh
West Lulworth
Buckland Newton
Puddletown
Higher Bockhampton
Chaldon Herring
Durdle Door
Folke
Holnest
Cerne Abbas
Dorchester
Whitcombe
Poxwell
Bincombe
Ringstead
Isle of Portland
Sherborne
Thornford
Dorchester
Upwey
Weymouth
Southwell
Portland Bill
Lewcombe
East Chelborough
Maiden Newton
Littlebredy
Chesil Beach
Corscombe
Beaminster
Netherbury
Symondsbury
Bridport
Burton Bradstock
Abbotsbury
Broadwindsor
Chideock
Seatown
Lyme Regis

The Faerie Dance

The fairies dance the wild dance
When moonbeams flood the earth,
Jumping, leaping nimbly
Upon their sacred turf.

Round and round they circle
In a wreath of shimmering light,
The merry revellers dance away
Through out the Summer night.

A wanderer might be drawn
Inexorably towards the ring,
But just one foot placed inside
And the Faerie dance will bewitch him.

The fairies dance the wild dance
Mortals should stay clear,
Enchanted though for an instant
Brings death within the year!

Robert Newland

Introduction

The word 'fairy' is believed to derive from the old French *'Fae'* or *'Fay,'* which derived from the classic *'Fatae'* - the Fates who preside over man's destiny.

The word *'fairy'* itself was probably introduced to Britain by the Normans, but it wasn't until the Tudor period, when the persecuted French Protestants, *The Huguenots* came over to England to settle, that the word *'fairy'* became commonplace. Shakespeare helped popularise the change, which in time replaced the old Anglo Saxon 'ELF' to make 'FAIRY' the standard term for all elementals, sprites, goblins, nymphs and nature spirits.

It is very hard to distinguish one type of fairy from another yet this has not prevented numerous scholars of fairyology dividing fairies into species and subspecies, which in itself is complicated and confusing.

Many fairyologists overcome this by choosing the easy option classifying fairies by whether they are *solitary fairies* or trooping fairies. However, though this might seem an accurate way to class fairies, it is really much too vague. Others choose to categorise fairies by their habitat, location or the four elements, all of which become contradictory.

Therefore for this short guide of Dorset fairyology I have chosen to divide up the fairies into five classic types:

Flower Fairies
Sprites
Nymphs & Nymphets
Ignis Fatuus
Goblins & Bogeys

This I hope will make Dorset fairy classification less complex and at the same time make fairies easier to identify should anyone encounter them.

Robert Newland
www.darkdorset.co.uk

The Fairy Phenomenon

Of all the supernatural phenomena, the 'fairy' seems about the most unlikely. We even use the expression 'fairy stories' to describe obvious lies. Yet there are people even today who are firm believers in fairies, some even claiming to have seen them or have heard the soft strands of fairy music. Fairy legends and fairy encounters alike are told the world over, but it is here in the British Isles where the fairy phenomenon is strongest.

"It is hard for the mind to grasp what the ultimate results may be if we have actually proved the existence on the surface of this planet of a population which may be as numerous as the human race, which pursues its own strange life in its own strange way, and which is only separated from ourselves by some difference of vibration."

Sir Arthur Conan Doyle: *The Coming of the Fairies*

FAIRY APPEARANCE

Fairies vary region-to-region and indeed encounter-to-encounter, however, it is not uncommon for the fairy appearance to reflect our own preconceptions of them. The most popular fairy form is female, ether naked or clothed in green, white or red, sometimes with the addition of a cap. Male fairies can also appear either naked or clothed but they tend to be ugly and grotesque in comparison and more dwarf-like in stature.

Smaller fairies are often characterised with a pair of wings, while larger fairies cannot be distinguished from humans. Yet fairies have been known to appear as dancing flames, and beasts such as shaggy colts with red fiery eyes. Fairies can appear beautiful or ugly, in troops or just on their own, but when they appear it is usually without warning and they disappear just as quickly.

FAIRY ORIGIN

Explanations for the fairy phenomenon are as varied as the fairies themselves. Serious scholars of fairy lore have suggested that fairies are in fact a distant folk memory of a pigmy-like prehistoric race, which once co-existed alongside humans. Other suggestions say fairies are fallen angels, or the remnants of old pagan gods, or even the spirits of the heathen dead which were not good enough for Heaven and not bad enough for Hell, so they exist in a sort of limbo here on earth. An example of this exists here in the West Country where tradition tells us that pixies are the souls of un-christened children.

One controversial modern day theory is that fairies are aliens from other worlds or different dimensions. This could indeed be the case if you happen to believe in aliens visiting Earth. There are however similarities between both fairies and aliens. Aliens and fairies are often described as *'little green men',* and both are blamed on creating strange circles in grass and crop, and both are in the habit of abducting people.

SEEING FAIRIES

Whatever the real fairy origin, it is generally thought that fairies exist on two levels. When fairies are visible they are on the ETHERIC level, (a state more subtle than gaseous) and when invisible they are on the ASTRAL level, (a state finer than Etheric). It is believed that fairies can change levels at will but it is only on the Etheric level that they can be seen.

I know a bank whereon the wild thyme blows,
Where oxlips and the nodding violet grows;
Quite overcanopied with luscious woodbine,
With sweet musk-roses, and with eglantine:
There sleeps Titania some time of the night,
Lull'd in these flowers with dances and delight;
And there the snake throws her enamell'd skin,
Weed wide enough to wrap a fairy in:

William Shakespeare: *A Midsummer Night's Dream*

Growing children, particularly girls just prior to puberty are far more likely to see fairies than adults. The reason put forward for this is that children, especially girls, are more receptive and that puberty is an unstable border line between childhood and adulthood.

Borderlines are particularly relevant where fairy sightings are concerned. According to fairy lore, midnight and midday, sunrise and sunset, and the night of the full or new moon, are the most likely times to encounter these elusive beings. To add to this there are a number of days in the year when fairies seem particularly active.

These are as follows: *Candlemas or Imbolc, 2nd February; The Feast of Diana, 12th February; The Spring Equinox, 21st March; Walpurgis Night, 30th April; May Day or Beltane, 1st May; The Summer Solstice, 21st June; Midsummer Eve, 23rd June; Lammastide, 1st August; The Autumnal Equinox, 23rd September; All Hallows Eve (Hallowe'en) or Samhain, 31st October; The Winter Solstice, 21st December; Christmas Eve, 24th December; and New Year's Eve, 31st December.*

As favourable as these dates and times may be, fairies tend to be very choosy to whom they make themselves visible. Sometimes no amount of residing in misty forest glades, or upon moonlit barrows, or indeed any other number of favourite fairy haunts, will reveal anything but a sense of damp. In truth fairies are more likely to be found over the next rise or under the next leaf, for those that seek to find fairies will rarely do so.

On the other hand, those not looking for fairies might idly stumble upon them without even realising. It must be said now that the real fairy experience is very different from the stereotypical story book view of delicate creatures with gossamer wings and happy endings, so popularised by Victorian and contemporary writers alike. In reality an encounter with fairies is fraught with danger and one should think him or herself very lucky indeed if one emerges unharmed.

At this point it is worth noting that when dealing with fairies one must not take anything for granted for only one thing is certain and that is - nothing is certain! All offers of kisses, food and drink should be refused, for any mortal foolish enough to kiss a fairy, drink or eat fairy food will become enchanted. This might take the form of a deep sleep, forgetfulness, a longing for more fairy tastes, or one might be led into continuous enslavement, or even to an early grave!

Little Fairy Kiss-Kiss,
Cease the breath of Little Miss.

PRACTICAL JOKES

It is a noted fact that all fairies love nothing more than to make sport with unsuspecting humans. Their practical jokes are often spiteful and dangerous though rarely life threatening. Their favourite trick is *'Pixy-leading'* unwary travellers, ie, to be misled by fairies either by light at night or by a subtle changing of landmarks and features by day.

Fairies also take great pleasure in punishing the greedy, lazy and dishonest by pinching them black and blue.

Shee, that pinches countrey wenches
If they rub not cleane their benches,
And with sharper nayles remembers,
When they rake not up their embers.

Ben Jonson: *Entertainment at Althorpe*

Many ailments and diseases were once believed to be caused by fairies; rheumatism, miscarriages, slipped discs and in particular strokes. A stroke was thought to be caused by a fairy throwing *'fairy-shot'*, ie, sharp fragments of stone that when hit the body would cause the victim to suffer a sudden paralytic seizure. Wasting diseases, and consumption too, were blamed upon fairies and were attributed to joining in fairy revels.

My mother said I never should
Dance with the fairies in the wood;
If I should, she would say,
Naughty girl to disobey

Traditional Nursery Rhyme

FAIRY HAUNTS

Contrary to popular belief fairies prefer windswept hills and wooded dells than the shady nooks at the bottom of the garden, which is said to be the haunt most favoured by fairies. Ancient earthworks, stone circles, and barrows in particular are by tradition the homes of fairies and it was believed that such earthworks were gateways to Fairyland.

"The fairies usually took up their abode during the day underground in the bosom of isolated round green hills... indeed almost every circular mound must once have been used thus, if all tales be true."

Folklorist William Brockie 1886

One could find the hidden entrance by running clockwise, nine times around a barrow without drawing a breath at midnight on the night of the full moon. If this couldn't be achieved one could wait until the night of Lammastide (1st August) when it was believed that all fairy barrows rose up on pillars and revealed the way to Fairyland, but only the foolish dared enter.

Fairies often go to great pains to protect their barrows and gold. Treasure seekers and those choosing to build on fairy terrain may be warned by strange voices, baleful sounds and even sudden storms. Should such warnings be ignored, ill luck, disaster and even death will be the only reward.

All fairy haunts like Fairyland are enchanted and magical places that are full of hidden danger. Anyone who idly invades a fairy haunt may suddenly be overcome with dizziness and hear peals of discordant laughter. Unless they at once turn their pockets and coats inside out - a sure way of breaking fairy enchantment - they will be pixy led, and wander aimlessly lost for possibly hours. Some may be attacked by swarms of invisible fairy fingers pinching them all over while others may suddenly be struck with overwhelming despair or unexplainable fear. However, some might not be so lucky, for they may become enchanted and spirited away never to be seen or heard of again.

Invitations to visit fairy haunts should be taken with extreme caution, yet witches are said to be frequent visitors to fairy haunts, one of the many accusations made at them during the witch trials of the seventeenth century. So many old crones and young girls alike, most of whom were entirely innocent, were sent to the ducking stool or burnt at the stake, solely on the evidence given by malicious neighbours reporting them for visiting fairy haunts and consorting with fairies.

FAIRYRINGS

All fairies whether good or evil, enjoy dancing in circles in the grass. This has given rise to the popular belief that fairy circles or *'fairyrings'*, as they are often called are brought about by fairies dancing.

> *"But zome,*
> *Do zay do come by lightnèn when do thunder;*
> *An' zome do zay sich rings as thik ring there is,*
> *Do grow in dancèn tracks o' little veäries,*
> *That in the nights o' zummer or o' spring*
> *Do come by moonlight, when noo other veet*
> *Do tread the dewy grass but their's, an' meet*
> *An' dance away together in a ring."*

William Barnes: *The Veäries*

The wild enchantment of fairy music can lead an unwary victim inexorably towards the circle and to imminent doom. From outside the ring the fairies often remain invisible, however, should the victim be tempted to step inside the circle he or she would suddenly be plunged into a whirl of frenzied dancing. Bewitched and unable to escape the ring's enchantment, the poor soul would be forced to join in the fairy revel. What happens then is something of a mystery, but it is believed the fairies steal part of the victim's soul or character before turning the unfortunate person out of the ring.

> *Come follow, follow me,*
> *You fairy elves that be:*
> *Which circle on the greene*
> *Come follow Mab your queene,*
> *Hand in hand let's dance around,*
> *For this place is fairye ground.*

Anon

If the victim is fortunate enough to have a quick thinking companion he or she may be pulled out before any damage is done, but any helpers must keep one foot outside the ring or they too would be drawn into the fairy revel. A glove turned inside out and tossed into the ring will scatter the fairies and thus help aid a rescue.

However, joining in fairy revels poses enormous risk, for like fairy food and drink, once someone has experienced a fairy revel they will only want more. An inner compulsion will draw the victim back to the original ring time and time again, but his or her fate would already be sealed. The victim would survive after being returned by the fairies but only a shadow of his or her former self. The unlucky man, woman, boy or girl would become gaunt and pale, and hover in a meaningless sort of half-life for some weeks or months before eventually dying from no obvious cause.

CHANGELINGS

Perhaps the most disturbing habit fairies have is that they often abduct human babies and leave a fairy *'changeling'* in their place. The changeling may be an old ugly elf or even a baby carved of wood, but under fairy enchantment or so called *'Fairy Glamour**, it appears to be an exact replica of the stolen child. For what purpose the child is taken is unclear, but one suggestion is that every seven years the land of *'Faerie'* pays a tithe (Tiend) to Hell and the human captives are used as payment.

'And pleasant is the fairy land,
But, an eerie tale to tell,
Ay at the end of seven years
We pay a tiend to hell;'

Francis James Child: *Tam Lin*

Other suggestions for child abduction include: to strengthen the dwindling fairy stock, or to use them as slaves and entertainment for the Faerie Court. However, a fairy changeling would be a weak sickly thing, and would eventually die but the unsuspecting parents would hold a funeral for maybe nothing more than a block of wood. Those parents who discovered the changeling's true identity and cared for it would rarely be rewarded. It was believed the only way to rid oneself of a fairy changeling and retrieve one's own child, was to treat the changeling with extreme cruelty. Once the changeling had gone the human child would often be found on the doorstep.

The Fairy Crime

When the unchristened child lies asleep
Into the nursery the fairies creep
By the troop they come a flocking
And do some thing most shocking
In an instant they steal the bonny child away
And leave behind a changeling to stay.

Whether it be a replica carved of wood
Or whether it be a goblin with rattle and hood
The only way to get the stolen child back
Is to put the changeling into a sack
And hanging it from a tree
Beat it without mercy
A just and fitting punishment for this crime
When beating the sack repeat this rhyme.

With switch and stick and cane
I'll beat you again and again
I'll beat you and make you flee
Bring back my child to me.

And by being so unkind
The next morning one should find
Upon the step outside the front door
The human child once more.

Robert Newland

Children are not the only members of society at risk of fairy abduction. Beautiful women and handsome men along with poets, writers, artists, musicians and sculptors are all at risk, for fairies seem to be attracted to all manner of artistic creation.

* Fairy enchantment that deceives by appearance, hence ugliness is seen as beauty, vice-versa pebbles as money etc.

PROTECTION

Wise country folk have for generations used numerous methods of protection against troublesome fairies.

A four-leaf clover or the turning of pockets and clothing inside out is a certain way to break fairy enchantment, while iron, such as a nail or a horseshoe (moon symbol) hung above an entrance is considered very effective against fairies gaining access.

A cross marked on a cake is believed to stop fairies dancing upon it, and red ribbons, open scissors, and daisy chains (sun symbol) are used to prevent fairy abduction. Bread is yet another powerful protection, for even just the mere mention of it can break fairy enchantment.

Another form of protection is a 'hag stone', 'holy stone' or 'witch stone' ie, a smooth beach pebble with a natural hole through it. Looking through a hag stone will break fairy glamour. Such stones are also believed to prevent nightmares and the bewitchment of livestock, especially horses; incidentally hag stones were once widely used as a charm against witchcraft.

Anything to do with Christianity; the Bible, holy prayers, holy water, cross or crucifix, and even churchyard mould are all considered strong protection against fairies and other evils. Bells too, are considered effective against fairies, for it is believed their ringing disturbs the atmosphere in which fairies have their incorporeal being.

Other forms of protection include; salt, a twig of broom, a banishing pentagram ie, drawn anticlockwise, shoes or socks placed under the bed with the toes pointing outwards, flax on the floor, a pig's head drawn on a door, and the midsummer flower St John's wort.

SUMMARY

All in all, when pleased, fairies can be overwhelmingly generous, rewarding those in their favour with gifts of money and much good fortune, but equally when angered they can bring misery, ill luck and disaster. One must remember an encounter with fairies is heavily laden with danger and extreme caution needs to be taken at all times. Respect and goodwill towards fairies is the best policy to adopt which in turn might bring bountiful rewards, but woe betide anybody taking liberties; - they might never return alive!

Introducing the Fairies of Dorsetshire

We are the Little Folk - we!
Too little to love or to hate.
Leave us alone and you'll see
How we can drag down the Great!
We are the worm in the wood!
We are the rot in the root!
We are the germ in the blood!
We are the thorn in the foot!

Rudyard Kipling: *The Pict Song*

Flower Fairies

The loveliest and daintiest of all fairies are the small flower fairies whose task is to care for all growing things.

Smiling little fairy
Climbing up the stem
Tell us which is prettiest?
She says, "All of them!"

Cicely Mary Barker: *The Song of the Phlox Fairy*

Most people perceive flower fairies as the classic *'Tinker bell'* type, much like those drawn by Cicely Mary Barker, of sweet pretty little girls dressed in petals with butterfly wings. This in itself is not incorrect but flower fairies are not as sweet and as innocent as they may appear. Their temperament can be as changeable as the weather being kind one moment and spiteful the next. The flower fairies of Dorset are called *'Pillywiggins'* and like all other fairies they are not to be trusted.

'Pinch him, pinch him, blacke and blue,
Sawcie mortals must not view
What the Queene of Stars is doing,
Nor pry into our Fairy woing.'

John Lyly: *Endimion*

Little Neighbours

A legend is told that long ago on one bright summer's morning a woman baked a cake and left it to cool down outside upon the kitchen windowsill. Moments later much to her surprise she heard the faint sounds of merry laughter and so with curiosity looked out of the window to see who was giggling. To her utter disbelief there dancing upon the cake were a number of little Pillywiggins, all with golden hair and beautiful blue wings. Anxious to speak with them the woman said, *"Hello Little Neighbours!"* at which all the fairies instantly vanished into vapour and disappeared.

The Secret Gift

From the Irish leprechaun to the modern day tooth fairy, fairies everywhere have always been associated with hidden treasure and gifts of money. This too applies to the Pillywiggins who have been known to bestow gifts of money.

At the turn of the twentieth century, Miss Caroline Gooderson, a respectable God-fearing woman of Maiden Newton, once had her young niece and nephew, Kitty and Billy, to stay at her cottage.Miss Gooderson was unprepared for them as the arrangement was very sudden, but she made them feel welcome as best as she could. Every day the children would go out to play in the nearby fields and meadows only to return about an hour later in fits of giggles with secret smiles on their lips as if they had something to hide.

Miss Gooderson didn't think much about it; they were children after all. However, one afternoon when she was cleaning in the children's bedroom, she discovered under the bed, a small box containing a number of gold coins. Astonished at the find she came to the conclusion that the children had stolen the money. When Kitty and Billy came back for supper Miss Gooderson confronted them both with the hoard. *"Wer did thee zeal these?"* she said firmly. But Kitty and Billy refused to say where they got the money.

"If thee don't tell, I'll have thee over me pinner* and make thee smert with a withy!" warned Miss Gooderson.

"Plea don't make us tell thee." said Kitty in alarm. *"We promised not to tell but I swear we didn't zeal it!"*

Miss Gooderson was not in the mood for nonsense and decided to beat the truth out of the pair of them.

Soon Kitty could stand the thrashing no longer. *"The veäries in the honeyzuck gid it to us!"* she said tearfully.

"Yes twere the veäries gid it to us," said Billy. *"And now we have told, we shan't be gid any more!"*

Miss Gooderson didn't know what to believe, but when the unpleasant business was over she sent the children straight to bed. However, she soon discovered that the box containing the gold hoard, which she had left on the kitchen table had gone. Miss Gooderson looked high and low for it, but it was nowhere to be seen; it had just simply vanished! No doubt reclaimed by the Pillywiggins for breaking a promise.

* pinafore

Fairy-locks

The Hawthorn tree is a favourite of the Pillywiggins for they love to dance in its shade. Anyone foolish enough to rest under such a host tree may find themselves pinched by tiny fingers, or lulled to sleep only to re-awake to find that the Pillywiggins have plaited their hair full of tangles, otherwise known as *'fairy-locks'*.

Two little sisters living in the village of Sturminster Marshall in the 1890s had a case of fairy-locks. The incident happened one May Day afternoon when the girls, tired and exhausted from all the Maypole Dancing and other seasonal celebrations, rested under a Hawthorn tree. They hadn't been there long when their sparkling eyes closed and they drifted into a deep sleep.

When the girls awoke they discovered that they were covered from head to toe in painful red blotches, but worse still, their hair was so tangled and knotted it was impossible to comb out; so all their fairy-locks had to be cut off!

The 2004 Sturminster Marshall May Day celebrations.

The Fairies' Death Bell

Flowering Blue Bell woods are particularly treacherous, as the Pillywiggins love to ring the Blue Bells. It is said that if you hear the chime of a Blue Bell, you are hearing your own funeral bell summoning you to your grave hence they are often called *'Fairy's Death Bells'* and *'Death Bells'*.

Death's Chime

Oh woe if you hear the Blue Bell,
Its toll is heard deep within ones heart,
Oh woe if you hear the Blue Bell,
For you will soon depart.

Oh woe if you hear the Blue Bell,
It tolls for both young and old,
Oh woe if you hear the Blue Bell,
For you will soon be left cold!

Robert Newland

Sprites

The word sprite can be used to describe any type of fairy but on the whole sprites are a mixture of different fairies varying in character, appearance and size. They are the little people of the toadstools, wee folk and little green men of meadow, hill and woodland glade, which do not fit the description of any of the other four fairy types. They are quite simply *'miscellaneous fairies'*.

Oh! prythee come and dance with me
Around the ring where fay
And elfish sprites in revelry
Their nightly gambols play.

Traditional Rhyme

White, Green & Black Fairies

On the 20th August 1566, John Walsh of Netherbury appeared before the Bishop of Exeter accused of practising witchcraft. John Walsh confessed that he frequently visited fairy barrows between the hours of twelve midnight until one in the morning, and twelve noon until one in the afternoon, where he would speak with white, green and black fairies. He also claimed the fairies told him about the people bewitched in the village and he added that the black fairies are the wickedest.

Fairies, black, grey, green, and white
You moonshine revellers, and shades of night.

William Shakespeare: *The Merry Wives of Windsor*

Guardians of Hillock & Hill

On Bincombe Hill overlooking Weymouth can be seen six fairy hillocks that date back to the Bronze Age. They were known locally as *'Music Barrows'*, for it was said if you put your ear to the top of one at noon, you would be able to hear the plaintive tones of music. Such fairy music is known to be beautiful and capricious. It has a fatal charm to mortal ears, for even just a few notes may lull the listener into a fatal sleep, or they might become drawn into a melancholic forgetfulness, always yearning to hear more.

In recent memory, an unknown woman visiting the village asked if fairies really did live under the bumps and if, indeed, music could be heard. She was warned to stay well away from the barrows, but was seen going up the hill that morning, never to be seen or heard of again.

The Bincombe Music Barrows.

There was an old woman lived under a hill,
And if she's not gone, she lives there still.

Traditional Nursery Rhyme

The lure of hidden fairy treasure once led two men in 1621 to a barrow within the parish of Upwey near Weymouth. They were soon to be disappointed for after three days of hard digging they turned up nothing but a few bones. It was later rumoured by the villagers that both men died before the year was out.

According to legend there is a fairy barrow at Milborne St. Andrew which is said to hide much treasure, including a solid gold coffin, but past attempts to remove it have always resulted in failure, for every time anyone goes to dig for it, there is thunder and lightning.

Fairy Voices

Not that long ago a woman wanted to purchase a plot of land closely adjacent to the tree-covered music barrow, *Culliford Tree*, at Whitcombe, for the purpose of building her house there. She was said to have visited the barrow on two occasions to make up her mind whether to buy the land or not. On both visits she heard a sinister voice warning her to desist from her plan. After the second visit she wisely changed her mind and cancelled the project.

Opposite Culliford Tree there is a smaller barrow known as *'The Singing Barrow'*. It was at this barrow in 1983 that two friends heard a strange humming, whining noise. It did not come from any one point in the barrow, but the so-called singing seemed to be coming from all around it.

The Ballard of Culliford Tree

Behold Culliford Tree. - The piper of the noon
The regal green monarch of solstice June
Its crown of beech reaches up to embrace the Summer sky
Where all about swallows swoop, low and high
Virgins come, but never leave its shady bowers
The innocent victims of nature's powers
A loving embrace serenaded by the sweet sound of the lark
Who whispers sweet nothings of hearts carved in the bark
The death of virginity is announced by the jay
New birth is but nine moons away!
But yet there is still a strange tale to tell
For magical energy flows through this ancient bell
And deep within its pregnant belly dome
Can be heard, so some say, an eerie tone
A trill note piercing below ground
A most uncanny peculiar sound

Robert Newland

The Pixies' Barrow

Pixies were once encountered at *Bottlebush Down,* which lies between Sixpenny Handley and Cranborne. The Reverend Bruce of Sixpenny Handley was a keen amateur archaeologist and as such he would often be found after the Sunday church service on Bottlebush Down making notes about all the earthworks there.

On one occasion he had been out much later than usual so he decided to rest on one of the many Bronze Age barrows, and watch the sunset before making the long trek back home. It was a beautiful sunset, the air was still and in the southwest the new moon rouse a silver sickle. Yet as he stretched out he suddenly became aware of something moving close beside him. Looking to see what it was, he was astonished to see countless little pixies dressed in leather jerkins dancing in a circle around him. For several minutes he watched in total disbelief then in a blink of an eye they all vanished. No doubt he probably visited the barrow many times after the encounter, but one suspects the pixies never showed themselves to him again.

> *By the moone we sport and play,*
> *With the night begins our day;*
> *As we daunce, the deaw doth fall;*
> *Trip it little urchins all,*
> *Lightly as the little Bee,*
> *Two by two and three by three:*
> *And about go wee, and about go wee.*

Anon

Fairies Extinct

There was once a fairy barrow at a place called *Folly Hanging Gate* at *Washers Pit* in Ashmore, which the villagers said was inhabited by strange fairy-like spirits called *'Gabbygamies'* or otherwise *'Gappergennies'.* For countless generations anybody visiting the barrow would be rewarded by the hypnotic sounds of the Gabbygamies within.

However, in 1840 the barrow was levelled to make way for a new road. Some human bones were found in the heart of the mound and these were later buried in the churchyard. With the barrow gone, the uncanny sounds of its inhabitants were never heard again.

The Fairy Market

Dorset's most beautiful and famous hill Golden Cap at Seatown is popular with tourists and walkers alike, yet just a stone's throw away to the northeast is the solitude of the wooded summit *Langdon Hill.* Perhaps because of its over-shadowed nature the fairies have made it their home.

On one unaccountably cold Christmas Eve night, a poor man down on his luck was making his way home on horseback after attending Midnight Mass at St. Gabriel's Church. The man was miserable, cold and hungry and he cursed his bad luck and the chill air that nipped his fingers, and in his utter despair he cried out into the darkness, *"Curse my life for poverty!"*

Making haste in the darkness he soon skirted below Langdon Hill and along Pettycrate Lane where he saw, looming through the fog, all lit up with light, a fairy market taking place.

It was like any other market, there were pies and cakes, fruit and vegetables, and all manner of fine things for sale. Taken with curiosity, he urged his old nag on unnoticed by all the sprites hustling and bustling, busy buying and selling their wares to all manner of devils and witches!

Suddenly the man caught sight of a small sack bursting with gold coins. This was an opportunity too good to miss!

Unphased by the fairies and the evil all around him he spurred his horse on through the throng, and as quick as a flash, seized the sack and galloped off for dear life, and did not stop until he was safely back home.

Laughing with glee at his good fortune, he rushed into his old tumbledown cottage eager to count the stolen loot, but on opening the sack he discovered to his bitter disappointment all the money had been changed into small pebbles. The gold money was just *'fairy glamour'.* How he cursed the fairies for their trickery, but this didn't help matters, for he remained poor and miserable for the rest of his days.

Could make a ladye seem a knight,
A nutshell seem a gilded barge
A sheeling seem a palace large
And youth seem age and age seem youth
All was delusion, nought was truth.

Reginald Scot: *The Lay of the Last Minstrel*

The Fairy Bell Ringers

The Christian Church considered all fairies to be the servants of the Devil and strived to drive them back to Hell by way of holy prayers, holy water, holy bread, crosses and the ringing of church bells. Yet there are fairies who, no matter what, still linger on and show their defiance against Christianity.

Stourpaine Church.

The fairies of *Hod Hill* near Blandford are no exception, for it is believed they ring the bells of Stourpaine's Holy Trinity Church when the morning dew is on the grass. This they do by entering the bell tower through the small external doorway or priest's door dubbed *'The Fairy Door'* and climb the stone staircase to the very top where they softly ring the bells by urinating over them. Yet if anyone should enter the church they might just see the fairies inside swinging on the bell ropes laughing.

The door used by the fairies to gain access to the bell tower.

How they clang, and clash, and roar!
What a horror they outpour
On the bosom of the palpitating air!

Edgar Allan Poe: *The Bells*

The Offended Fairies

About a mile northwest of Evershot is the church-less village of East Chelborough. The reason exactly why a church was never built there lies hidden beneath the summit of *Castle Hill,* where a medieval castle was once sited.

Early on in the sixteenth century the population of East Chelborough had grown so much that a church was needed in the community for worship. After some debate a space was chosen in a field by the road at the bottom of Castle Hill, but as the residents could not afford professional stonemasons they decided to undertake building the church themselves.

No one seemed concerned that fairies inhabited Castle Hill, few even considered the matter at all, and so the villagers started work on their much-needed church. They began digging the foundations and laying the first large stones of the walls, and when the first day's work was over, all the people went home pleased with how much they had done.

However, that night as the villagers slept the fairies in troops came out of Castle Hill and took great offence at what the residents of East Chelborough had done. The fairies did not want a church built at the bottom of their abode, so they picked up every stone block and with cries of *'Horse and Hattock'** flew northwards until they came to the parish of Lewcombe and the river there.

The fairies of Castle Hill were earth beings and therefore could not cross over the river, so they dumped the blocks down in a great heap before returning back to Castle Hill.

The next morning the people of East Chelborough soon discovered what the fairies had done, but they were confident Christianity would triumph over these soul-less beings and in turn would drive them away. A horse and cart was sent to fetch the blocks and the people of East Chelborough started work on the church again. They made an enormous effort, almost building half the church that day, and when they went home they all agreed not even the Devil himself could move so much stone in one night.

How wrong they were, for that night the fairies came out of Castle Hill and did exactly as before. They removed all the stone blocks and dumped them back by the river at Lewcombe.

* The magic words said to be used by fairies to aid the flight of Shift-horses - ie, stems of Ragwort or Rye Grass that fairies sometimes ride through the air in much the same fashion as a witch would use a broom.

31

On the third day the people of East Chelborough began to lose faith, but still they made one last half-hearted attempt to build their church and at the end of the day went home tired and wondering if their efforts would still show in the morning.

That night the fairies did the same, once more dumping the stone blocks back at Lewcombe. The following day the people of East Chelborough gave up. They decided to build the church at Lewcombe by the river.

In time the population of East Chelborough declined and no attempt to build another church there was ever made, but the church of St. James at Lewcombe remains there to this day and as for the fairies of Castle Hill - who knows?

The quaint little church at Lewcombe surrounded by peace and tranquillity.

More Churches Moved

The church at Holnest and the one at Folke, (both near Sherborne) have very similar legends to that of Lewcombe. Both churches began their construction in *Broke Wood,* but what was built during the first day was carried to its present position during the night by fairies.

The Fairy Revel

Anyone driving along the A35 between Bridport and Chideock can't help but notice the tree-topped landmark *Colmer's Hill,* which overlooks the village of Symondsbury. In 1816, when Colmer's Hill had yet to acquire its trees, there lived in the parish of Symondsbury a pretty nine-year-old girl called Ann Ward.

The foreboding conical shaped hill at Symondsbury where malevolent fairies are believed to reside.

One day when Ann was playing alone in the fields below Colmer's Hill she heard the faint sounds of strange bewitching music drifting on the breeze. Curious at this she followed the sound, which soon led her to a fairy ring. It looked like any other fairy ring but the very moment Ann stepped inside the circle, she found her self in a whirl of dancing fairies.

Within moments she became intoxicated with the hypnotic flow of rash music, which seemed to be rising from out of the ground and as if drawn against her will, she began to dance. Ann danced and danced until suddenly without warning she was tossed up into the air and fell back down all in a heap just outside the fairy

ring and in that instant the music ceased. Tired and exhausted Ann staggered home, but didn't tell anyone about her experience.

The next day Ann rushed off to the fairy ring and again she danced with the fairies, and as before she was soon tossed out of the ring, exhausted and gasping for breath.

Day after day she went back to the ring to dance with the fairies, only to return home with her clothes all dishevelled and torn and a noticeable far away look in her eye.

In time Ann grew thin and listless and her mother, suspecting that her daughter was partaking in fairy revels, one day decided to follow her. At length she saw Ann as loose-jointed as a scarecrow dancing wildly inside the fairyring. She dared not go closer, but on Ann's return, made her promise never to go near the circle again. However, the next day Ann did go, and when she didn't return for supper, her mother went to look for her. Sadly she was too late. Ann's lifeless body was found lying just outside the fairy ring; apparently she had been danced to death!

Pan Pipes

More fairy music was heard at Colmer's Hill in September 1939. A class of school children was on a field trip there when they heard a *'haunting melody of pan pipes'* coming from deep within the hill's summit. The unusual music caused so much fear and distress that the class left immediately.

The windswept pine trees at the summit of Colmer's Hill where uncanny fairy music was once heard.

The Little Intruder

The Second World War brought another fairy encounter to light, which otherwise might have been lost forever.

In 1939 Dot Pickford was evacuated from London and was billeted out to stay with a Mr and Mrs Coombs of Dorchester. Living at the house with them was Mrs Coombs's mother; a very old jolly woman of at least ninety years of age and who was known to one and all as "Old Mother". It was Dot's first time away from home and understandably she was very homesick, so to cheer her up Old Mother would often tell her a story or two.

One day the old woman recounted a story, which had been told to her several times when she had been a young girl; the story of when her Grandmother saw a pixie.

When her Grandmother was a young woman she worked at a farm situated in the *Marshwood Vale,* west Dorset. One summer morning she was alone in the kitchen busy preparing lunch for the labourers who were in the fields gathering in the harvest, when all of a sudden the kitchen door, which was ajar, was gently pushed open and in walked an instantly recognisable little pixie. He was thin, greenish in colour with a distinct turned-up nose, large pointed ears and a squint, about a foot high, dressed in a bottle-green jacket and tight-fitting pantaloons and a red conical hat, which was extremely twisted and bent at the tip. His feet were bare and large and very noticeably out of all proportion with the rest of his body.

Blinking in amazement she remained perfectly still and silent and watched with a great degree of curiosity the actions of the little intruder. The pixie walked over to the stove and began to scrutinize the various objects there; the large bubbling pot of stew, the steaming kettle, the poker and coal scuttle.

It was evident to her that the pixie was unaware of her presence. Slowly taking his time he made his way over to a large dresser whereupon were plates, jugs and cups. He paused for a brief moment before the kitchen clock ticking loudly on the wall caught his eye. The little fellow stood gazing up at the clock, which had a large face and a swinging pendulum, and with slow deliberate movement he began to sway to and fro in relation to the pendulum. This amused him very much and he began to mumble to himself. Suddenly the clock began to chime noon. The pixie, startled at this, gave a loud shriek and darted out through the door from which he came and was never seen again.

The Wild Hunt

Amongst the rolling hills of west Dorset about five miles northeast of Bridport is the notorious fairy haunt, *Eggardon Hill.*

The bleak windy summit of Eggardon hillfort where a host of unfriendly demons and fairies ride in search of lost human souls.

It is by far one of the finest examples of a hillfort anywhere to be found in the county. It began as a Neolithic settlement and developed through the Bronze and Iron Age only to be raided and captured by the Roman Second Augustan Legion in 43A.D.

Anyone who has ever spent an hour on a windy day there will realise why so much superstition and folklore has grown up around the hill.

One legend says: At night when the grey mist veils the Downs or when the winds roar, one might see Diana the Moon Goddess, leading her ghostly wild hunt of fairies, demons and witches over its summit collecting the souls of the dead.

Mysterious Eggardon Hill

The Mysterious fortress Eggardon Hill,
Where sky-clad witches gambol still
Dancing in hag tracks upon the windswept fell
Making magic and enchanting spell.
Far above through purple skies
On pale lunar light flies
Diana, the host of the Wild Hunt
With devil dogs at the front,
A crescendo of demons and fairies eagerly pursuing
The souls of the dead over the ruin.

Robert Newland

Dancers on the Lawn

Several sprites were once seen in the early part of the twentieth century by a Mr Lonsdale and his friend, Mr Turvey, a gifted clairvoyant, in a garden on the *Branksome Park Estate,* Bournemouth. Mr Lonsdale wrote a detailed account of his fairy encounter, which appears in Sir Arthur Conan Doyle's book: The Coming of the Fairies.

"We sat in a hut which had an open front looking on to the lawn. We had been perfectly quiet for some time, neither talking nor moving, as was often our habit. Suddenly I was conscious of movement on the edge of the lawn, which on that side went up to a grove of pine trees. Looking closely, I saw several little figures dressed in brown peering through the bushes. They remained quiet for a few minutes and then disappeared. In a few seconds a dozen or more small people, about two feet in height, in bright clothes and with radiant faces, ran onto the lawn, dancing hither and thither. I glanced at Turvey to see if he saw anything, and whispered, 'Do you see them?' He nodded. These fairies played about, gradually approaching the hut. One little fellow, bolder than the others, came to a croquet hoop close to the hut and, using the hoop as a horizontal bar, turned round and round it, much to our amusement. Some of the others watched him, while others danced about, not in

any set dance, but seemingly moving in sheer joy. This continued for four or five minutes when suddenly, evidently in response to some signal or warning from those dressed in brown, who had remained at the edge of the lawn, they all ran into the wood. Just then a maid appeared coming from the house with tea. Never was tea so unwelcome, as evidently its appearance was the cause of the disappearance of our little visitors."

The Portland Fairies

The Isle of Portland was once a popular fairy haunt, for the fairies lived amongst the *Nether Field* of the old open field system, where they were often to be seen on moonlit nights dancing in the many toadstool rings.

However, according to local legend, in the 1750s when the new church of St George was built and its bells first rang out over the island, all the fairies fled in terror along the Chesil Beach and were said to have never returned. Yet since then it is believed that some fairies have indeed returned and dwell on the island once more.

The view from Portland of the Chesil Beach where the fairies were seen fleeing from the chime of the first church bell.

39

Nanny Diamonds

On Portland in the neighbourhood of Southwell, fairies known as *'Nanny Diamonds'* haunt the road that leads to Cheyne.

Their name has no doubt been corrupted over the years. *'Nanny'* probably comes from *Nanoid;* meaning *'dwarf-like'*, while *'Diamonds'* could be a corruption of *Diana*, ie, Diana the Moon Goddess.

The Nanny Diamonds wear short white dresses and white Phrygian hats, and on still moonlit nights can be observed sitting and dancing on top of the dry stone walls on either side of the road. Though they seem quite cute and friendly, they are not to be trusted for they have the power to bestow the *'Evil Eye'*, and love nothing more than to lead people astray with forbidden fruits and promises of love and untold riches.

However, between the hours of twelve noon and one in the afternoon the Nanny Diamonds can be bribed into granting wishes by hiding a silver coin among the nooks and crannies in the walls.

The road and wall frequented by the Nanny Diamonds.

ᘒ𝓃ymphs & ᘒ𝓃ymphets

The numerous classes of beautiful semi-divine fairy maidens of human height, inhabiting the seas, rivers, springs, meadows and woods etc, are known collectively as *nymphs*. Most nymphs are indistinguishable from humans, although their enchanting beauty and erotic charm set them apart. The nymphs who dwell in the water are far more dangerous than their cousins who dwell on land for no matter how beautiful and graceful water nymphs may appear, all are characterised by a morbid and uncontrollable sexual desire. With their seductive charm they entice mortal men into their element where in an orgy of carnal lust they murder them.

BEWARE!

Beware! Of that lonely forest pool,
For shameless beings live there,
Maidens so beautiful to see,
Maidens so sweet to hear,
Beckoning you to caress and kiss,
Invitations to do what you wish.

But! Beware! Human they are not,
For they are water nymphs, a
treacherous lot,
Cold webbed hands with an iron grip,
Will drag you down into the water pit,
Under the water and into the gloom,
Down and down to meet your doom!

Robert Newland

Oreads, the nymphs of the mountains and caves can be equally dangerous for they can inflict madness upon any mortal man, sometimes causing them to jump to their death from high craggy cliffs.

Wood nymphs on the other hand can drive men to despair. A wood nymph either lives in a tree, in which case she is called a *Hamadryad* or close to it and is therefore called a *Dryad*. A Hamadryad's well-being depends on the tree that she inhabits; should her tree be cut down or die, then she would die also. This indeed seems to be the case for all breeds of nymph. Destroy the habitat in which they exist and they too will cease to exist!

Nymphs are classified by the type of habitat in which they dwell, deriving their names from ancient Greek. For example, the nymphs of the mountains are called *Oreads,* acquiring their name from the Greek word for mountain, *"oros".*

Nymph Classification

NYMPHS OF SPRINGS & RIVERS
Naiads

Sub Class
Limniads (Lakes)
Potameides (Rivers & Streams)
Crinaeae (Fountains)
Pagaeae (Springs)
Eleionomae (Marshes)

NYMPHS OF THE SEAS & OCEANS
Nereids (Mediterranean sea)
Oceanids (Oceans)

NYMPHS OF THE AIR
Sylphs

NYMPHS OF FIRE
Salamanders

NYMPHS OF THE MOUNTAINS & GROTTOES
Oreads

NYMPHS OF THE VALLEYS
Napaea

NYMPHS OF THE MEADOWS
Limoniads

NYMPHS OF THE WOODS &TREES
Dryads & Hamadryads

Pools of Doom

A quarter of a mile southeast of Hardy's cottage at *Thorncombe Wood,* Higher Bockhampton, there is a circular pool called *Rushy Pond.* Local legend says: The pool is inhabited by beautiful water nymphs that lure unwary travellers into the pool, never to be seen again.

The silent still waters of Rushy Pond, where beneath its reflection dwell beautiful but sinister maidens.

Mother may I go and bathe?
Yes, my darling daughter
Hang your clothes on yonder tree,
But don't go near the water.

Traditional Nursery Rhyme

Not far from Old Harry Rocks at Studland there is another mysterious pool whose level is said to never change despite storms and droughts. The pool is believed to be the home of yet more water nymphs which, on moonlit nights, emerge from the depths to come on land and dance.

Also, close to a footpath that leads towards the sea at Ringstead, near Weymouth, there is another pool with exactly the same legend.

The Kiss of Death

Not far from Wool, sited on the banks of the river Frome, is the now ruined Cistercian monastery Bindon Abbey.

Long before its dissolution, there lived a twelve-year-old boy called Lubberlu who would earn extra money for his family by running errands for the monks.

Sometimes while on an errand Lubberlu would walk along the banks of the river and on hot days go swimming.

One particularly warm summer's day Lubberlu was doing just that when out from the bulrushes appeared the most beautiful girl he had ever seen. Her blue eyes sparkled like the sunlight on the water and her silvery hair cascaded like a waterfall. She beckoned Lubberlu to come to her side and kiss her! Captivated by her beauty, Lubberlu instantly stepped forward and kissed her on the lips and at once became enchanted. All that morning he laughed and talked to the girl, but soon it was time to go. The girl kissed Lubberlu and made him promise to return the next day and return he did. And the day after, and the day after that! Lubberlu spent many days in the company of the mysterious girl who had captured his heart, for he was head over heels in love.

Autumn approached and Lubberlu told a monk at the abbey all about the girl saying how one day he wished to marry her. As Lubberlu spoke more about the girl the monk soon realised that the girl was not an ordinary mortal but a nymphet of the river!

Between the age of nine and fourteen there occur maidens who, to certain bewitched travellers, twice or many times older than they, reveal their true nature which is not human, but nymphic (that is demonic); and these chosen creatures I propose to designate as 'nymphets'.

V. Nabokov: Lolita (1959)

He knew that Lubberlu was in serious danger for it would only be a matter of time before she revealed her true murderous nymphic nature to him and told Lubberlu to keep away from her. There could never be any happiness! When Lubberlu heard this he was horrified. In tears, he ran as fast as he could to the river calling for the girl.

He was never seen alive again! A few days later Lubberlu's dead body was found tangled among the bulrushes, floating face down in the river. He had been drowned at the hands of the young nymphet!

The river Frome at Wool where a young boy was once believed to have been murdered by a beautiful young water spirit.

The Dance Macabre Maidens

Lulworth Cove is a geological marvel and a perfect natural harbour. Its circular shape surrounded by high cliffs is truly an impressive sight, therefore it's no wonder that Lulworth Cove has become a busy tourist attraction.

Yet during the mid-1930s when Lulworth Cove was a peaceful fishing village a retired naval commander, who was single-handed sailing along the Dorset coast, sort refuge in the cove for the night.

After a trip ashore for provisions he rowed the short distance back to his converted lifeboat. With the sunlight fading, the silent, deserted cove took on a bleak and dismal appearance, but once thankfully below in the warm cabin he lit up the oil lamps and started work on his unfinished manuscript. About an hour had passed when suddenly the peace was broken by *'singing'.* The commander slid back the companion hatch and stood listening for a few moments at what he thought was someone on shore with a radio. However, as he reached to close the hatch a *'wild crescendo of screams'* tore across the night air. He leaped up the companion ladder, his heart in his mouth, and desperately sought to penetrate the wall of darkness. The shrieking inferno raged all about him for what seemed like a lifetime when abruptly the screaming stopped and the cove was deathly silent once more.

Suddenly he saw from out of the water the tiny figure of a young nymphet walk up onto the shingle beach. The sight of her pale expressionless face and dripping body rising from the waves chilled his blood in an instant.

Lulworth Cove where the mysterious dancing nymphets were first encountered.

Once on shore she began to dance a strange jerky, macabre type of dance. Suddenly another nymphet appeared from out of the water and then another and another until there were about a dozen willowy nymphets, all dancing an utterly joyless dance - *'The Dance of Death'.* His heart thumping in his chest, the commander stood frozen with fear watching this strange mournful travesty of a childhood game.

Many moments passed, then without warning and all at once, the nymphets went still as if they had been restrained by a deathly-unheard command. Gradually they all grew faint and disappeared, leaving the curved beach just as before and leaving the retired naval commander in a state of abject terror.

It would seem that this stretch of Purbeck coastline is often frequented by these dancing nymphets for the area called *The Fossil Forest,* just east of Lulworth is often called *'The Fairy*

Dancers'. And further east there is a rocky platform called *Dancing Ledge*. However, going west just past Durdle Door there is a stretch of beach backed by high cliffs called *Bat's Head*. It was there in 1994 these enigmatic sea-maidens were encountered once again, this time by husband and wife, Mr and Mrs Baker from Poole. Mrs Joan Baker sent to me a detailed account of her fairy encounter.

"In February 1994, my husband and I decided to go for a walk along the coast at Durdle Door. It was a bleak wintry day and it was trying to rain but we made our way down the steps and on to the beach where we were greeted by the famous arch. We were the only people there, which made it very peaceful and pleasant. As we made our way further along the beach towards Bat's Head beach I suddenly noticed, about fifty yards ahead, a group of about ten young girls about the age of nine or ten all of which were stark naked and walking towards the sea as if about to go swimming. Most were blond, but all had pale white skin. I nudged my husband. "My goodness, they're brave!" I said. My husband looked up and he saw them too. "They must be foreign students or something," he replied. We watched somewhat bemused as they walked out into the cold surf but then we looked away back towards Durdle Door to see if there was anyone else on the beach behind us also witnessing this heart-warming exhibition of childhood innocence. But when we looked forward again, all the girls had gone from our sight. We had only glanced away for a brief moment! We rushed along the beach to the very spot where they had only just been seconds before, but they were nowhere to be seen. We looked out to sea and searched all along the beach to see if we could find any of the girls' belongings. We searched thoroughly along the whole of the beach, even inside a little cave at the base of the cliff, but we found nothing! It all seemed very strange."

The beach at Bat's Head, west of Durdle Door where a number of mysterious young sea-maidens were recently encountered.

The Circle of Enchantment

In the early part of the twentieth century a Mr J. Foot Young had an encounter with nymphets at *Okeford Hill* at Okeford Fitzpaine. He wrote to Sir Arthur Conan Doyle telling of his encounter.

"Some years ago I was one of a party invited to spend the afternoon on the lovely slopes of Okeford Hill, in the county of Dorset. The absence of both trees and hedges in this locality enables one to see without obstruction for long distances. I was walking with my companion, who lives in the locality, some little distance from the main party, when to my astonishment I saw a number of what I thought to be very small children, about a score in number, and all dressed in little gaily-coloured short skirts, their legs being bare. Their hands were joined, and all held up, as they merrily danced round in a perfect circle. We stood watching them, when in an instant they all vanished from our sight. My companion told me they were fairies, and they often came to that particular part to hold their revels. It may be our presence disturbed them."

Okeford Hill where a fairy revel was once witnessed.

Merry Maidens

Following the Okeford Hill incident there has been a number of other similar fairy sightings at various locations around the county.

Near Winterborne Stickland there is a wood known locally as the *fairy wood*. It acquired its nickname when a Mr Dominic French claimed he had once encountered there a troop of dancing, colourful semi-transparent maidens about four feet tall.

At Langton Matravers during the 1970s, green-skinned nymphets wearing red Phrygian hats (the cap of Liberty) were reportedly seen dancing in the twilight near *Wilkswood Farm* in *Langton West Wood*. At about the same time in the west of the county beautiful alluring nymphets with dark brown hair were seen dancing on the tree-covered slopes of *Lewesdon Hill* near Broadwindsor.

Since the 1970s nymph and nymphet sightings have continued for they have been allegedly seen dancing at the *Five Marys* barrows near Chaldon Herring, at *Maiden Castle* near Dorchester and at *Kingston Russell Stone Circle,* not far from Littlebredy.

The steep ramparts of Maiden Castle, Britain's largest Iron Age hillfort.

Ignis Fatuus

A phosphorescent flickering light or ball of fire seen hovering or flitting over marshland and sometimes graveyards is called 'Ignis Fatuus' which literally means 'foolish fire'.

If approached they often recede and finally vanish only to reappear in another direction, therefore if followed they seem to purposely mislead. This led to the popular belief that the lights were caused by a mischievous fairy intent on leading travellers into pools, ditches and quagmires.

If any wanderers I meet,
That from their night-sport do trudge home,
With counterfeiting voice I greet,
And cause them on with me to roam;
Through woods, through lakes,
Through bogs, through brakes,
O'er bush and brier, with them I go,
I call upon
Them to come on,
And wend me laughing, ho, ho, ho!

Ben Jonson: *Carew Hazlitt's Fairy Tales, Legends and Romances Illustrating Shakespeare*

Country folk have given the Ignis Fatuus phenomenon numerous names including: Kit with the Candlestick; Joan the Wad; Fairy Fire; Corpse Candles; Spunky; Fetch Candles; Hob and his Lantern; Death Fire; Pinkets; Foolish Fire; Hinky Punk; Jill O' Wisp; Fox Fire; Hobby Lantern; William with the little flame; Friar's Rush; Fairy Sparks; Marsh Fire; Pixie Light; Ghost Lights; Jenny Burnt Tail; Dead Men's Lights; Peg O' Lantern; Pretty Polly; Wandering Jack; Hell's Fire; The Lantern Man; Dancing Flames; Flickering Fanny; Old Woman of the Mountains; Phantom Lights; Puck or Puxey Light; Moor Lights; Water Sherie; Graveyard Guardians; Elf Light; Billy with the Wisp; Death Flame; Fire Damp; Fair Maid of Ireland; Wild Fire; but most people call it *Jack O' Lantern* or *Will O' Wisp*.

Foolish Tom

Once in the north of the county (exact location unknown) there lived a young shepherd boy called Tom.

One cold and misty winter's night Tom was sent out to look for a missing ewe, which was soon to lamb. Tom searched and searched for a very long time, but it was so dark and foggy he couldn't find her anywhere. Just as he was about to give up and turn for home, he was suddenly startled by the appearance of a strange flickering light moving close to the ground just a little distance away. Tom was very curious at this and without a second thought gave chase.

The light bobbed this way and that way and though Tom ran as fast as he could, he was unable to catch up with it. Soon he found himself running on soft boggy ground, but still Tom ran on after the light. Then without warning he ran straight into a quagmire and immediately became stuck fast. Suddenly there was an evil laugh and the light went out. It was only then that Tom realised he had been tricked, - pixy led by Jack O' Lantern.

Tom shouted for help as loud as he could, but nobody heard his cries until the next morning when he was rescued and severely reprimanded for his foolish folly.

Man a-lost!

Another classic Jack O' Lantern encounter happened in west Dorset in the mid-nineteenth century.

Jonathan Albert, a labourer who worked for the Mabey family of Beaminster, would often turn up for work late in the morning saying he had seen Jack O' lantern on his way home and had got lost.

His fear of meeting Jack O' Lantern was so very real that on some nights he refused to go home at all and would spend the night in the Mabey's hay loft. However, on one such night he felt something pass over him three times. He dared not open his eyes for he knew it was Jack O' Lantern trying to bewitch him. Yet on the third time Jonathan did open his eyes and saw to his horror a vision of his sister holding up her hands and blood streaming down, and by her side was Jack O' Lantern. The next day he heard that his sister had been murdered!

Three days after his sister's funeral, Jonathan was walking home in the evening gloom when he saw Jack O' Lantern in a wood. Bewitched once again by the bobbing light he followed it and soon fell into a water filled ditch, but in trying to get out he only went in deeper and deeper. In his utter despair he called out into the darkness. *"Man a-lost!"* to which the doves in the wood replied, *"Who?"* to which he answered, *"Jonathan Albert, as good a man as ever bought a loaf of bread!"* And at that he somehow managed to scramble free from the ditch and went home.

And leading us makes us to stray,
Long winters nights out of the way,
And when we stick in mire and clay,
Hob doth with laughter leave us.

Michael Drayton: *Nymphidia*

The Burning Fairy Barrow

High upon the downs of Ridgeway Hill, Bincombe, there is a bowl barrow known locally as *'The Burning Barrow'*.

It was given this name due to an unexplainable event one night in the early 1980s. A woman, who was riding pillion on the back of a motorbike, was with her boyfriend travelling along the top road of Came Down, when the rider and herself were both startled to see flames shooting upward and a bright orange glow emitting from one of the many barrows upon the Ridgeway. Both the rider and the woman thought the area had some sinister air about it and didn't stop to find out what caused this unusual phenomenon. However, what they might have seen was dancing fire fairies!

Laughing Will O' Wisp

Mr James Pullen of Thornford once had an encounter with a Will O' Wisp that he heard laugh, while walking home from work one very cold evening in November 1984.

"I had just got off the train at Thornford Station and was walking briskly along the lane back to Thornford. It was dark as the lane is unlit by streetlights, and it was very cold as I recall. I had not walked barely halfway when I heard in the darkness ahead of me what sounded like a trill of laughter. I stopped at once and at that moment I saw, scarcely ten paces before me, a ball of red light about the size of a tennis ball, come floating just off the ground, out from the hedgerow, cross the road and disappear through the hedge on the other side, where I distinctly heard it laugh again. As you can imagine I didn't stay to see if it came back, but hastened my step until I was home!"

The Dance of Jill O' Wisp

Little Jill O' Wisp leads the merry dance
Over marsh and mire,
Leading wayfarers off the path
With her wisp of fire.

Leaping nimbly over toadstools
Little Jill dances swiftly,
Through the rushes and the bog grass
Where the ground grows shifty.

Come, come and dance with me
Jill's flames beckon and call,
But those foolish enough to do so
Will be led into a bottomless pool.

Robert Newland

Goblins & Bogeys

The word *Goblin* was first recorded as early as the twelfth century by Ordericus Vitalis who mentioned *Gobelinus* as a popular name of a spirit which haunted the neighbourhood of Évreux, France.

By the sixteenth century the usage of the word goblin had become widespread and then, as today, mainly refers to the ugly, grotesque impish elves and fairies.

Goblins are at best devilishly tricky and at worst downright evil. Those that are considered evil tend to go to great lengths to do harm. They mainly prey upon the weak and vulnerable often tempting them with forbidden faerie fruits, with the purpose to lead astray or to an early grave.

Goblins are the companions to the dead; this is particularly true on Hallowe'en when they gather in graveyards to feast ghoulishly upon decaying corpses. But worse than this, some goblins invade honest households seeking out naughty young girls and boys to eat alive! Such Goblins are called *'Nursery Bogeys'* and their names were often used as threats to ensure good behaviour.

Molly had a baby
She dressed it all in green
Molly didn't want it
*So she left it for the queen**
The queen did not like it
Because it was always sobbing
So she cut it up in slices
And fed it to a goblin.

Traditional Nursery Rhyme

Cornish children feared a visit from *Bloody Bones;* Somerset children feared *Tankerabogus;* but Dorset children feared the *Spoorn!*

*The queen of the fairies

The Spoorn

During the latter half of the nineteenth century there lived at the village of Corscombe an eleven-year-old girl called Mary Marsh who worked as a lowly kitchen girl at a busy farm.

In those days it was common practice for children to be contracted out for employment to escape the harsh reality of poverty. Like so many children of the time, Mary probably had a miserable existence working in drudgery for long hours, and undoubtedly she was mistreated and underfed.

Beware the Spoorn, - the child eater
Hungry for young tender flesh.
Hurry! Hurry! Bolt the door shut
And lock the windows tight
For the Spoorn is out to feed tonight!

Robert Newland

One Hallowe'en night Mary was alone, working late in the kitchen when she was startled by the sudden appearance of an ugly little goblin upon the windowsill outside. It was what most Dorset children feared - the dreaded goblin called *The Spoorn!* However, Mary was unaware of this and so with curiosity asked him what he wanted. The Spoorn complained of the cold and begged Mary to let him inside so he could warm himself by the fire. Mary was a kind-hearted girl and taking pity on the little fellow she opened the window and let him into the kitchen.

For sometime the Spoorn warmed himself by the iron range and when he had warmed himself enough, he produced a fat juicy pear and gave it to Mary as payment for her kindness. *"Take it!"* said the Spoorn, *"If you dare. It won't hurt you, I swear!"* But the pear was a magic pear, for when Mary took a bite she fell unconscious on to the floor.

It was all a wicked trick for while Mary slept the Spoorn helped himself to a tart, baked that day by the farmer's wife. The tart filled his goblin tum, so much so that he decided not to eat Mary after all. The Spoorn, chuckling to himself, opened the window and ran away into the night.

The farmer's wife found Mary the next morning asleep on the

floor and shook the poor girl from her slumber accusing her of eating the tart. Of course Mary denied it and said it was the goblin and not she. But adults know best and rarely believe in such things as goblins! And so Mary's explanation fell on deaf ears. The blame was firmly put on Mary for the Spoorn's thieving and as such poor Mary was severely punished with a vigorous spanking.

We must not look at goblin men,
We must not buy their fruits;
Who knows upon what soil they fed,
Their hungry thirsty roots?

Christina Rossetti: *Goblin Market*

Poke or Puck

Sometimes the names given to certain places, barrows and other monuments give a clear indication to the type of fairies or indeed goblins that haunt them.

The village of Poxwell, near Weymouth, used to be called Pokeswell until 1906. The name refers to the word *Poke* or *Poker,* which is by definition a name often given to a breed of mischievous goblin. A variant of this is *Puk* or *Puck,* the hobgoblin made so very popular by Shakespeare.

I am that merry wanderer of the night:
I jest to Oberon, and make him smile,
When I a fat and bean-fed horse beguile,
Neighing in likeness of a filly foal:
And sometime lurk I in a gossip's bowl,
In very likeness of a roasted crab;
And, when she drinks, against her lips I bob,
And on her whither'd dewlap pour the ale.
The wisest aunt, telling the saddest tale,
Sometime for three-foot stool mistaketh me;
Then slip I from her bum, down topples she,
And "tailor" cries, and falls into a cough;
And then the whole quire hold their hips and loff,
And waxen in their mirth, and neeze, and swear
A merrier hour was never wasted there.

William Shakespeare:
A Midsummer Night's Dream

Puck is often called *'Robin Goodfellow',* yet his character is far from good, for he loves to jest and play mean tricks upon anyone he should encounter, hence his name has been given to numerous places where no doubt some unfortunate soul became sport for his impish mischief. Poxwell is one prime example of this, for legend says that such a puck haunts *Moigns Down* at the spot where the five footpaths meet and should any loan traveller stop there for even just a brief moment he will become pixy led.

Similar legends exist at Sturminster Newton where there is a *Puxey Coppice* and a *Puxey Lane:* and at Langton Matravers where there is a farm called *Putlake,* which used to be called Puck Lake, (lake referring to a stream in this case). On Godlingston Heath at Studland one can find the *Puck Stone,* near Winfrith Newburgh there is a barrow called *Puckysbury Barrow,* and at Puddletown there is a place called *Puck Pit.* The sea on the western side of The Cobb at Lyme Regis is known as *Poker's Pool,* while at Bournemouth there is an area of the town called *Pokesdown.*

The list can go on with yet more different goblin variants such as *Grimberry Barrow* at Corfe Castle, and *Bug Barrow* at Bere Regis. However, the eroded long barrow *The Grey Mare and her Colts* near Littlebredy probably acquired its name from the bogey beast the *Colepexy,* an altogether different breed of goblin.

The Puck Stone on Godlingston Heath lies almost hidden amongst the heather and gorse.

Poke Ridden

Pucky, Puck, you mischievous Poke,
You love to jest, you love to joke,
But I'm tired of your spiteful tricks
All of which put me in a proper fix!

You play your pranks by the score
But I can stand it no more!
You chimed the clock before the hour
And you turned the milk sour

You upset the milk pail
The cream you gave to the cat
You pulled the stool from under me
Just as I sat

You pinched me hard
When I was sweeping the step
You told aloud
All the secrets that I kept

You ripped my Sunday frock
When I went through the lich gate
Then you led me astray
And I arrived home very late

You gave me a rash
Which caused much unpleasant itching
I turned my back for a moment
And you had unravelled my knitting

I was threading the needle
And you pricked my thumb
Then you sent a bumble bee
To sting me on the bum

You scalded me hot
When I was bathing in the tub
And when I jumped out
My big toe you did stub

You blew out my candle
Leaving me in the dark
Then you kept me awake all night
By making the dogs bark

You hid my clothes
I was unable to dress
You kicked over the chamber pot
It was a terrible mess

Yesterday in the kitchen
At me you threw copper pots
And now this morning
In my hair I find fairy-locks

I'm so tired and weary
I'm bruised purple, black and blue
To escape your attentions
I know now what I have to do

I will knock a nail in the door cold
And above it place ancient churchyard mould
And with a cross, read the 23rd Psalm
All of which will keep me from harm.

So whether you haunt from hob to hearth
Or from creamy churn to old tin bath
You little Poke will have to flee
Far away and gone from me!

Robert Newland

The Colepexy

Somewhere roaming the beautiful downs of Dorset is the mischievous goblin colt with flaming red eyes called the *Colepexy.* His name literally means *'Conjuring Pixie',* which by his very nature is to trick and deceive his victims.

This Puck seems but a dreaming dolt,
Still walking like a ragged Colt,
And oft out of a Bush doth bolt,
Of purpose to deceive us.

Michael Drayton: *Nymphidia*

The Grey Mare and Her Colts long barrow where possibly the Colepexy emerged from.

Some accounts say his coat is jet black, while others claim it's grey, but whichever, he is a shape-shifting bogey beast who loves nothing more than to *pixy-lead* domesticated horses and travellers and to scare people - particularly children.

Once a gypsy woman, who as a child lived with her family in a caravan at a site known as *Burgess Field,* Parkstone, near Poole, claimed that during the light of day, her brother and herself, while in the caravan, were visited by a horse-like devil. She described the fiend as *'a black, velvety thing with wild flaming red eyes and flaring nostrils'*.

The two children sat huddled close together terrified of the creature that was leering over the half door of the caravan. They called out for their parents in desperation, who were only just outside the caravan, but they saw nothing of the fairy creature. They searched the area but found nothing, not even any hoof prints on the ground outside. It had simply vanished!

It would seem the Colepexy has a fascination for caravans as he was up to mischief once again; this time at *Redlands Farm Caravan Site,* at Weymouth. The Bruce family from London were staying at the site in 1967 when early one morning Mrs Bruce was rudely awoken by something tugging off the bed covers. On opening her eyes she clearly saw the dark grey shape of a horse's head pulling at the sheets. Mrs Bruce immediately let out a loud scream, at which the creature vanished! There was a loud neigh and Mrs Bruce distinctly heard the sound of horse's hooves galloping away.

Throwing the Rider

The Colepexy also loves to lure unsuspecting people to ride him and once astride he takes them on a wild terrifying ride across the wettest and thorniest country before throwing them into a ditch or stream. This is known to him as: *'Throwing the Rider'*.

COLEPEXY'S COUNTRY

Seven little girls went a-walking,
In the Colepexy's country,
Playing hookey from their lessons,
They thought was very funny.

Dressed smartly in white pinafores,
With bows and frills to grace,
With smiles and mischievous grins,
Upon their pretty face.

Over gates and stiles they went,
Down many a winding track,
Exploring fields and pastures new,
Never once looking back.

Until they came to a hill side,
Where a shaggy grey colt they did meet,
"Hello there, pretty maidens fair!"
Was how the jade did greet.

"A talking horse, a talking horse!"
The little girls joyfully cried.
"May we get upon your back?
May we go for a ride?"

"Yes, climb up, climb up,
There's room for one and all,
Sweet little ones first,
Followed by the fair tall."

And by magic enchantment,
The colt lengthened his back,
And one by one the girls mounted,
To make the horizontal stack.

And when all were squeezed on,
Holding each other around the waist,
The fairy colt gave a wicked chuckle,
And down the hill he raced.

Galloping down into the valley,
Jumping many a dry stone wall,
The little girls held on tight,
For they did not wish to fall.

"STOP! STOP! STOP!"
The little girls frantically cried,
"We want to get off,
We don't like this ride!"

But the Colepexy just galloped on faster,
Paying no heed to their pleas,
Or their yells and cries,
Or their terrified screams.

Onward through briars and thorns he galloped,
Which tore their pinafores to shreds,
Through prickly gorse and stinging nettle,
That scratched and stung their legs.

Then at long last he threw the girls,
Head long into the River Frome,
Those bruised and scratched little girls,
Were soaked through to the bone.

And as the equine grey galloped away,
They heard him laugh, they heard him say,
"To ride upon a Pexy you must be a fool,
You seven naughty maids should be in school!"

Robert Newland

The Apple Thief

One good quality of the Colepexy is that he sometimes acts as a type of orchard guardian protecting apple orchards from thieves.

Once there lived in Wareham an old widow who owned two fine apple orchards, which were said to produce the best cider apples in Dorset. The old lady had a jealous neighbour who often thought about stealing her prize apples to make his own cider, though the thought of meeting the Colepexy prevented him. However, he was determined to rob her orchards, and this he planned to do by hiding in a large wicker basket, which he would make move by the aid of a magic spell he had obtained from a conjuror.

One September night he decided to put his plan into action, and climbed into the basket. He said the magic words and the basket bounded down the lane and straight into the widow's orchard. Once the basket had settled he murmured another spell and one by one the apples flew off the branches and began pelting the basket.

Suddenly one large apple smacked him straight in the eye; he leapt up out of the basket howling in pain and as he did so, felt sharp teeth sink into his backside. Without a second thought he fled the basket and ran for his life, but the Colepexy was quicker, he tossed the apple thief into the air, and as he fell to the ground the Colepexy kicked him in the back of his neck, snapping it in two and killing him instantly.

Early the next morning the widow found her neighbour's dead body next to his basket of apples with the imprint of a horse's hoof impressed on his neck, but the fairy colt was nowhere to be seen.

Colepexies Heads

Dorset country folk often called Belemnites - (the built shaped fossils found along the beach), *'Colepexies-fingers'* and fossil sea urchins, *'Colepexies-heads'*, for they were considered lucky. Elsewhere, fossil sea urchins were called *'Fairy Hearts'* or *'Fairy Loaves'*.

Jack and Gye went into the rye,
And they found a little boy with one black eye.
Come, says Jack, let's knock him down with a Colepexy head.
No, says Gye, let's buy him some fairy bread;
You buy him one loaf and I'll buy two,
And we'll bring him up as other folk do.

Traditional Nursery Rhyme

Author's Own Account

Over the many years during which I gathered information for this volume, I visited many of the known fairy haunts of Dorset. My aim being to complement the material already gathered with perhaps some up-to-date fairy encounters of my own. I knew that unlike clairvoyants and mediums my lack of etheric vision would hinder me in my task, but combining this with my age and the mere fact that I was looking for fairies, I came to the conclusion that an encounter would be very, very unlikely. Nevertheless with hope in my heart, an open mind and a flask of hot tea I went on my numerous expeditions. Eggardon Hill, Colmer's Hill, Okeford Hill, The Grey Mare and Her Colts, Lulworth Cove, Maiden Castle, Stourpaine Church, the churchyard at Corscombe, Rushy Pond, The Five Marys, Hanging Folly Gate at Ashmore, the banks of the river Frome and many others, all proved fruitless. However, at Bincombe Hill I did discover a large fairy ring, perhaps some evidence of fairies, but an encounter it wasn't.

Puck has fled the haunts of men:
Ridicule has made him wary:
In the woods, and down the glen,
No one meets a Fairy!

Lewis Carroll: *Puck lost and Found*

As time went on I began to have serious doubts whether I was ever likely to encounter fairies. Yet one damp October morning I decided to try my luck at Lewesdon Hill. The hill had an uncanny dream-like quality about it that day. The ethereal mist that enveloped the hill seemed to dance through the trees as if entangled in the deathly silence. There was something intoxicating about that silence which beckoned me to explore the hill thoroughly and when I came upon a wooded dell, I became bewitched in an instant. My heart became captured with enchantment and inspiration.

It seems totally incredible now that I may have actually encountered a dryad on those magical slopes yet the memories are blurred and the vision fades. Too much perhaps, yet I can scarcely believe it myself that I actually encountered her at all.

The Nymphet of Lewesdon Hill

A death shroud covered the beech wood hill,
Where Devil's spawn is scattered,
And autumn leaves crunch under foot,
The place where dreams are shattered.
Through the mist a far carrying call pierced the silent chill,
So sweet, it captured my heart and beckoned me up that hill,
I walked a well-worn path of folly,
Like many an enchanted before me,
But the surge of passion sped me on,
Onward, until I came upon a shaded wooded dell,
Where reclining on a mossy limb, was the Lewesdon girl-
An alluring nymphet, shameless without a care,
Naked open, laying bare,
And at once, I was caught in her nymphic snare.
Drawn by her dryad magnetism,
I kissed her moist lips so cold,
And ran my hands over her smooth body,
Exploring every curve, crease and fold.
Her girlish giggles led me on, her brown eyes full of desire,
And hot passion flared up into a penetrating, blazing fire.
We embraced a lover's embrace,
Until finally the passion that kindled,
Burnt away, and the flames of love dwindled.
The dying embers lulled me into a restless, but peaceful sleep,
Where I dreamed this girl so sweet, I would forever keep,
I eventually woke to find myself alone,
Freezing cold, chilled to the bone,
My heart sank, my dream ebbed away,
Taken forever, by that capricious forward Fay.

Robert Newland

Bewitching Lewesdon Hill.

However, where the magical enchantment of Faerie was concerned fate had one more trick up its sleeve.

On the 20th July 2001 I was driving home from Dorchester when my friend, who wishes to remain anonymous, suggested that as it was approaching noon, we should stop at Culliford Tree barrow to see if the legend of hearing music was true. I had listened to other barrows in the past but had heard nothing, why would this barrow be any different? But my friend was keen to give it a try, plus there was going to be a new moon that night, so I agreed.

With just a few minutes to spare we arrived at Culliford Tree and looking at our watches waited for the time to tick pass. As the seconds approached noon we put our ear to the top of the barrow and listened..........Nothing!.......... I was just about to give up when all of a sudden I distinctly heard what I can only describe as a high pitch tone like a sort of time signal inside the barrow. I shot up in utter disbelief. *"Did you hear that?"* Yes my friend had heard it too! I put my ear back to the barrow in anticipation of hearing more, but we heard no more *'music'*. We both left Culliford Tree amazed that the legend is indeed true and agreed that it was unexplainable.

Magical Culliford Tree with its crown of copper beech trees.

Some days later I went back to Culliford Tree and listened at midday again, but this time I heard nothing except the birds singing above and the odd passing car.

My only conclusion why this was so was that when we first listened to the barrow and heard its music, I whole-heartedly believed that I wasn't going to hear anything. Therefore by going back and expecting to hear it again, I heard nothing. As fairy lore states: *"Those not looking for fairies might idly stumble upon them, but those that seek out to find fairies, might never do so."* Nothing is evermore certain in the world of Faerie!

... you whose pastime is to make midnight mushrooms.

William Shakespeare: *The Tempest*

About The Author

Robert Newland was born in London in 1969 but has lived in Dorset since 1979. He has long been interested in folklore and legends and has written numerous articles on the subject for magazines and local newspapers. He is the co-author of Dark Dorset and the founder member of its sister website www.darkdorset.co.uk which is the only website devoted to Dorset folklore, legends, and mysteries.

In his spare time he likes to explore the countryside where he draws much of his inspiration. His other interests include Art, History, Writing, Poetry, Astronomy, Photography and British Flora and Fauna.

A Graphic Designer by profession, a published poet and his interest of folklore makes the author ideally qualified to write this book.

ACKNOWLEDGEMENTS

The Author wishes to express his gratitude to everyone who has helped in the compilation of this book.

Joan Baker, Christine Bruce, Merrily Harpur, Jeremy Harte, Mark North, James Pullen, Dot Smith, The Staff of the Weymouth Public Library, The Staff of the Dorset County Record Office.